with many a flirt and flutter
In there stepped a stately raven.

DEBATABLE DEATHS

UNSOLVED HISTORY

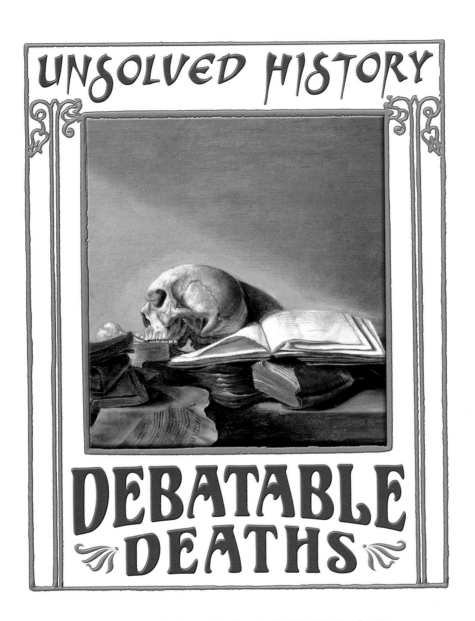

DEBATABLE DEATHS

GARY L. BLACKWOOD

Marshall Cavendish
Benchmark
New York

Marshall Cavendish Benchmark
99 White Plains Road
Tarrytown, New York 10591-9001
www.marshallcavendish.us

Book design by Michael Nelson

LIBRARY OF CONGRESS CATALOGING-IN-PUBLICATION DATA
Blackwood, Gary L.
Debatable deaths / by Gary L. Blackwood.-- 1st ed.
p. cm. -- (Unsolved history)
Summary: "Explores the mystery surrounding the deaths of various historical figures: Tutkankhamen, the
English Princes in the Tower, Christopher Marlowe, Mozart,
Meriwether Lewis, and Amelia Earhart"-- Provided by the publisher.
Includes bibliographical references and index.
ISBN 0-7614-1888-1
1. Biography. 2. Celebrities--Death. 3. Death. 4. Death--Causes.
5. Celebrities--Biography. I. Title. II. Series.
CT105.B583 2005
2004022237

Picture Research by Rose Corbett Gordon, Mystic CT
Front cover: Images.com/Corbis Back cover: North Carolina Museum of Art/Corbis Page i: engraving from
Poems by Edgar Allan Poe, Kegan Paul, Trench & Company, London, 1883; page iii: Musée des Beaux-Arts,
Caen, France/Giraudon/Bridgeman Art Library; page vi: Hamburg Kunsthalle, Hamburg, Germany/Bridgeman
Art Library; page viii: Mary Evans Picture Library/Institute of Civil Engineers; pages 2 & 42: Giraudon/Bridgeman
Art Library; pages 3, 45, 50, 52, 56 & 58: Corbis; page 5: Werner Forman/Art Resource, NY; page 6: Hulton-
Deutsch Collection, Corbis; pages 7, 27 & 60: Art Resource, NY; page 8: Royal Holloway, University of
London/Bridgeman Art Library; page 11: Syon House, Middlesex, UK/Bridgeman Art Library; pages 12, 13,
& 46: Mary Evans Picture Library; page 14: Christie's Images/Bridgeman Art Library; pages 15, 26, 28 & 33:
Private Collection/Bridgeman Art Library; page 16: Corpus Christi College/Bridgeman Art Library; page 18:
The Art Archive; page 19: Scala/Art Resource, NY; page 21: Kunsthistorisches Museum, Vienna/Bridgeman
Art Library; page 22: Birmingham Museums and Art Gallery/ Bridgeman Art Library; pages 24 & 48: Erich
Lessing/Art Resource, NY; page 30: New-York Historical Society, New York/ Bridgeman Art Library; page 34:
National Portrait Gallery, Smithsonian Institution/Art Resource, NY; page 36: Connie Ricca/Corbis; page 38
& 40: The Granger Collection, New York; page 42: Giraudon/Bridgeman Art Library; pages 54 & 57: The
Bettmann Archive/Corbis.

Printed in Malaysia
1 3 5 6 4 2

Front cover: *Man with Hands on His Face*, by contemporary artist Hillary Younglove
Back cover: *The Old Shepherd's Chief Mourner*, by 19th-century English painter Edwin Henry Landseer
Half title page: *The Raven*, 19th-century engraving for Edgar Allan Poe's famous poem
Title page: *Vanitas*, by 17th-century Dutch artist Jan Davidsz de Heem
Introduction: *Landscape with Grave, Coffin and Owl*, by 19th-century German artist Caspar David Friedrich

Contents

INTRODUCTION

*An unsolved murder does not really age. It continues to require
our attention, our questions, our unease.*
—Charles Nicholl

This is a book mostly about murder—or at least about suspected murder. Although the cases recounted here are definitely mysterious, don't expect them to resemble the traditional murder mystery. In a fictional "whodunit," the sleuth is generally presented with a corpse; by questioning witnesses and suspects and by carefully considering the clues, he or she cleverly deduces who the culprit is.

Investigating a death that happened many decades or many centuries ago isn't quite so straightforward. Since the suspects and the witnesses are generally dead as well, they can't be questioned; we have to rely on whatever testimony was written down at the time. But historical documents are notoriously unreliable, incomplete, and contradictory. Physical evidence is usually in short supply, too. The victim's body—if it can even be found—is at best a poorly preserved mummy and at worst a pile of bones.

Occasionally a fictional detective discovers that the victim wasn't murdered at all, that the death was due to an accident or natural causes. That may well be so in some of these real-life cases, too. Certainly many historians are content to believe that Meriwether Lewis killed himself; that Christopher Marlowe was slain in a quarrel over a tavern bill; that Amelia Earhart's plane ran out of fuel and went down in the ocean; and that King Tutankhamen, Prince Edward, Mozart, and Napoleon died of natural causes.

Unfortunately, once theories like these become accepted, it may be dangerous to question them. Anyone who seriously suggests some other, less conventional explanation runs the risk of being considered a bit of a crackpot, like those people who insist that the deaths of Marilyn Monroe, Martin Luther King, and Princess Diana are all part of some vast conspiracy.

But the fact is, the pages of history are positively packed with conspiracies. They're also full of murders that were passed off as accidents or natural deaths. There was a time when the accepted method for dealing with a rival or with someone who knew too much was to bump him off. (Actually, if you think about it, that method is still pretty popular.) It seems reasonable, then, when investigating a mysterious death from the past, to at least consider the possibility of foul play.

Besides, it's important to examine the past carefully from time to time, and question the conventional wisdom. As historian Audrey Williamson points out, "It is the questioners who have built and sometimes reformed our society, and from history we can always learn lessons."

The PHARAOH

AROUND 1550 BCE* THE RULERS OF EGYPT began building elaborate underground tombs for themselves in an area near Luxor now known as the Valley of the Kings. The burial sites were supposed to be secret, to prevent them from being broken into and looted, as the pyramids had been.

But when British archaeologists began digging up the tombs in the late 1800s, they found that nearly all had been plundered. Then, in November 1922, a former draftsman and tour guide named Howard Carter unearthed what one scholar calls "the richest discovery in the history of archaeology": a relatively undisturbed tomb that contained hundreds of priceless artifacts, some of them made of solid gold.

*Many systems of dating have been used by different peoples throughout history. This series uses BCE (Before Commion Era) and CE (Common Era) instead of BC (Before Christ) and AD (Anno Domini) out of respect for the diversity of the world's peoples.

Opposite: By the time Howard Carter began digging in the Valley of the Kings, most of the tombs had been cleaned out by archaeologists or by thieves. Carter's colleagues had given up on the area, believing that there was nothing left to find.

1

Among the treasures in Tutankhamen's tomb was this golden likeness of the pharaoh, which is now on display at the Egyptian National Museum.

It also held the mummified body of a young pharaoh (a title used by Egypt's kings) called Tutankhamen. So little was known at the time about him or his reign that Carter remarked, "Perhaps the most notable thing about Tutankhamen was that he died." It wasn't even clear how he died.

Since Carter's day, scholars and scientists have managed to fit assorted clues together to form a sketchy picture of Tutankhamen. It seems fairly certain that he was the son of Akhenaten, who is often called "the heretic king" because he rejected Egypt's traditional belief in many gods and worshipped only one, the sun god Aten. Akhenaten is an assumed name that means "it is beneficial to Aten."

Akhenaten's queen, Nefertiti, bore him three daughters. Tutankhamen (whose name was originally Tutankhaten—another tribute to the sun god) apparently had a different mother. When the boy was four or five, Akhenaten died. For two years the country was ruled by a shadowy figure named Smenkhare—some believe this was merely a "throne name" used by Nefertiti—and then Tutankhamen became pharaoh.

His chief adviser was Lord Ay (sometimes spelled Aye), Akhenaten's uncle. Under Ay's guidance the new king restored the traditional religion and changed his name to honor one of the old gods, Amen. He married his half sister, Ankhesenpaaten, who promptly changed her name to Ankhesen*amen.*

In 1323 BCE, Tutankhamen, then aged about seventeen, died unexpectedly. The tomb meant for him was still under construction, so his body was placed in a small tomb built for some less exalted person. Since he and Ankhesenamen hadn't produced an heir, Lord Ay took over the throne. Although he was far older than the widowed queen, he probably tried to reinforce his right to rule by taking her as his wife.

Ankhesenamen apparently wasn't willing; she sent this desperate plea to the king of the Hittites, Egypt's longtime enemies: "My husband is dead and I will not marry a commoner! Send me your son and I will make him King." Though Ay was the brother of Queen Tiye, Akhenaten's mother, he wasn't of royal blood, so he may have been the

If Tutankhamen hadn't died so young, he and Ankhesenamen might have produced a son who could have inherited the throne.

commoner she referred to. One of the Hittite princes, unable to refuse such an offer, set out for Egypt. Along the way he and his escort were attacked and killed.

A ring discovered in 1931 was inscribed with the names of Ay and Ankhesenamen linked together, indicating that Ay may have gotten his way despite the queen's objections. Some scholars suggest that, once she had served her purpose by strengthening his claim to the throne, he had her murdered.

If Ay really was that ruthless, it's natural to wonder whether he had some hand in Tutankhamen's untimely death, too. And in fact, not long after the boy king's body was discovered, Howard Carter's assistant speculated that Ay might have "arranged [Tutankhamen's] death, judging that the time was now ripe for him to assume the reins of government himself."

At that point, there was no real evidence that the pharaoh had been deliberately done in. It seemed just as likely that he had died from some disease, possibly tuberculosis. But in 1969, an X-ray of the mummy's skull revealed a thinning of the bone behind the left ear, perhaps the result of prolonged internal bleeding. "And this," said the pathologist who analyzed the X-rays, "could have been caused by a blow to the back of the head."

Naturally Ay was the prime suspect. But there were others, including a general named Horemheb, who took the throne after Ay's death. Horemheb so despised Tutankhamen and Akhenaten—whom he called the "Great

This mural from Horemheb's tomb shows the former general (*second from left*) keeping company with gods and goddesses.

Criminal"—that he tried to wipe out all record of their reigns. Apparently Horemheb's subjects considered him capable of the boy-king's murder, for he felt obliged to have a message carved into the base of one of his statues, proclaiming his innocence. "Egyptian brothers," reads one line of the inscription, "don't ever forget what foreigners did to our King Tutankhamen." He may have been pointing a finger at a court official named Tutu (or Dudu), who was a foreigner and something of a troublemaker.

Some experts dismiss the murder theory entirely. Egyptologist Christine El Mahdy considers it more likely that both the thinning of the bone and Tutankhamen's death were the result of a tumor. Someday, some new technology may determine the cause for certain. Until then, his case remains a bit of unsolved history.

The Pharaoh's CURSE

THE DISCOVERY of Tutankhamen's tomb caused a sensation throughout the world. It also caused a wave of panic, as rumors began to spread of a "pharaoh's curse." It all started when, during the excavation, Howard Carter's pet canary was swallowed by a cobra. Since the snake was a symbol of the pharaohs, the workers saw this as an evil omen.

The only warning Carter actually found inside the tomb was a mild one, carved into the base of a candle: "I am for the protection of the deceased."

Several months later *The New York Times* printed a letter from an American novelist, predicting doom for Carter and all his colleagues. The prediction was based on a quote supposedly found in an old Egyptian book: "Death comes on wings to him who enters the tomb of a Pharaoh."

Soon afterward Carter's financial backer, Lord Carnarvon, died in a Cairo hospital. The official diagnosis—a fever brought on by an infected mosquito bite—might have satisfied the public, except for two strange circumstances: At the moment of Carnarvon's death, all the lights of Cairo went out. At the same time, back in England, the lord's favorite dog let out a howl and dropped dead.

The notion of a pharaoh's curse gained ground when, over the next several years, more than twenty archaeologists and others who had visited the tomb were struck down, including American millionaire George Jay Gould and two of Carter's assistants. Terrified, hundreds of people who had brought antiquities home from Egypt as souvenirs hastily got rid of them. (As for Carter himself, although he suffered recurring bouts of illness, he lived to be sixty-six.)

Scientists offer several possible explanations for the premature deaths: bacteria or fungus in the tomb; the presence of radioactive material; or poison left there by the ancient Egyptians. But in 1980, the last surviving member of the excavation team revealed that Carter had started the "curse" story himself in an attempt to keep tourists and thieves away from the site.

Sir Arthur Conan Doyle, author of the Sherlock Holmes mysteries, theorized that the tomb was guarded by entities he called "elementals," supposedly created by Tutankhamen's priests.

The PRINCES

IN 1674, WORKMEN DEMOLISHED A STONE staircase in England's Tower of London. As they were digging up the foundations, they came upon a wooden chest containing the skeletons of two children. Everyone assumed they were "the bones of those two Princes who were foully murdered by Richard III."

The "two Princes" were the sons of Edward IV, an English monarch who had died nearly two centuries earlier. It was common knowledge that Edward's brother, the Duke of Gloucester—later King Richard III—imprisoned his nephews in the Tower and then ordered them killed, to eliminate any competition for the throne. But common knowledge is not the same as fact. The fact is, no one is really sure that Richard was responsible for the boys' deaths. As for the skeletons in the chest, it's possi-

Opposite: King Edward IV's sons were probably not as angelic as they appear in this 1878 painting, but they were by all accounts lively, intelligent, and charming.

9

ble that they're not really the remains of the princes.

This wasn't the first time, after all, that the "bones of the princes" had been found. In the early 1600s, what appeared to be a child's skeleton turned up in an underground pipe within the Tower. It proved to be the bones of an ape that had escaped from the Tower zoo. Around that same time period, workers broke through a wall in one of the Tower's passageways and discovered a hidden room. It held the skeletons of two children, aged about six and eight. This seemed to confirm the claim of a fifteenth-century chronicler who said that the princes had been sealed up in a secret chamber and left to starve. But the ages of the children were wrong; one of the princes was twelve and the other ten when they were killed—if they were, in fact, killed. There's some doubt about that, too.

The widely held belief that King Richard knocked off his nephews springs mainly from two highly subjective sources: Sir Thomas More's unfinished book *The History of King Richard III* and the play *Richard III* by William Shakespeare, who relied on More for his information. Sir Thomas was not exactly unbiased. He was writing during the reign of Henry VII, the man who overthrew Richard; it was clearly in his best interests to portray Henry's old enemy as an evil tyrant. Besides, there were some who suspected Henry himself of doing the boys in, and those suspicions needed to be put to rest.

There's probably no way we can ever know the whole truth of the matter. But, as historian Charles Nicholl says, "We can dig away some of the lies, and perhaps find beneath them a faint preserved outline of where the truth once lay."

Richard certainly wasn't the archvillain More and Shakespeare made him out to be. In fact, he was highly regarded by the common folk. His brother, Edward IV, trusted him enough to name him lord protector and guardian of the princes.

But when King Edward died in 1483, his oldest son—also named Edward—was in the care of the queen's brother, Lord Rivers. Fearing that Rivers would use his influence to seize power, Richard arrested him. Then he escorted young Edward to London, where he installed the boy in a part of the Tower that was used as a royal residence (another part housed prisoners of the crown). He also talked—or, some say, threatened—the queen into sending her other son (who was, confusingly enough, named Richard) to the Tower to keep Edward company.

It's uncertain whether or not Richard, the boys' uncle, had his eye on the crown at this point. What is clear is that he considered himself, and perhaps the princes, too, in danger from what he called the queen's "bloody adherents and affinity [relatives], which have intended . . . to murder

Sir Thomas More describes Richard III as having a hunched back and a withered arm. Contemporary portraits of him, though, show no deformity.

Although Prince Edward and his brother were closely guarded, Richard insisted that "he had not confined his nephew . . . rather he had rescued him."

and utterly destroy us . . . and the old royal blood of this realm."

Edward seems to have been a remarkably mature twelve-year-old. He was praised for his "virtuous disposition, his gentle wit and ripe understanding, far passing the nature of his youth." Even so, the common people felt Richard would make a better ruler. According to one writer of the time, they "began to support him openly and aloud: so that it was commonly said by all that the duke [Richard] deserved the government."

At the same time, a scandal surfaced that cast doubt on the crown prince's right to rule. The bishop of Bath revealed that before King Edward wed the queen, he had contracted to marry another woman. If this was true, it meant that the royal marriage was invalid and "that the children of King Edward IV were not legitimate, nor rightful inheritors of the crown." It also meant that Richard had no real need to get rid of the boys in order to become king.

When Richard was crowned in July 1483, the princes were undoubtedly still alive. According to the Great Chronicle of London, they "were seen shotying [shooting] and playng in the garden of the Towyr by sundry tymes." By the end of the year, though, it was being rumored that they "had died a violent death, but it was uncertain how." The chancellor of France was the first to openly accuse Richard—but far from the last.

DEBATABLE DEATHS

Few believed that Richard himself had done the deed. The most popular theory—and the one perpetuated by Shakespeare and Sir Thomas More—was that the boys were suffocated in their sleep by Richard's bodyguard, James Tyrell, with the help of two other men. According to More, they buried the bodies within the Tower, "at the stair foot, meetly deep under the ground, under a great heap of stones."

Richard was not the only suspect. One writer of the time was sure it was the Duke of Buckingham "who had put the two children to death, for Richard himself a few days afterwards ordered his execution." Of course, there was another reason for Buckingham's execution: he had just led a failed rebellion against Richard. If Buckingham had his eye on the throne, he may well have seen the princes as an obstacle. Certainly he would have had no trouble getting at them; as constable of England, he had easy access to the Tower.

Another person with a clear motive for murder was Henry Tudor, later Henry VII. As grandson of Henry V's widow, his claim to the throne was tenuous. But with young Edward and his brother out of the way, his chances would have improved considerably.

In 1485, Richard died fighting Henry's army at the Battle of Bosworth Field, and Henry became king. Naturally he encouraged the belief that Richard had "foully murdered" the boys. He had the Tower

Richard had little chance to show what sort of king he was. He ruled for only two years before he was slain at the battle of Bosworth Field.

Henry VII had to put down rebellions led by two different impostors, each claiming to be one of the princes.

grounds and buildings searched, but "the bones of the said children could never be found." It may be that, as More further claims, Richard had them dug up and reburied "in a better place, because they were a king's sons."

Or it may be that the princes were still alive. Rumors abounded, even during Richard's reign, that the boys were "living freely and securely . . . long after this murder was said to be done." According to a tradition handed down by the Tyrell family, far from being the boys' murderer, James Tyrell was their savior. Supposedly he spirited them off to his manor in Suffolk. Another account has them being concealed inside a wooden chest and smuggled off to Flanders.

A historian during the reign of Henry VIII noted that it was generally reported and believed that "the sons of Edward IV were still alive . . . and obscurely concealed in some distant region." Even Sir Thomas More admitted that "some remain yet in doubt whether they were in [Richard's] days destroyed or no."

But what about the two skeletons unearthed beneath the Tower stairs in 1674? Charles II, who was king at the time, declared them to be the bones of the princes and had them placed in a tomb in Westminster Abbey. In 1933, a pathologist and a dental surgeon got permission to examine the remains.

Some of the bones, they discovered, belonged to an animal. What remained were the incomplete skeletons of two children, one of twelve or thirteen, the other aged between nine and eleven. The doctors couldn't tell whether the children were male or female, nor could they determine the cause of death. They

did note that the older child had suffered from a severe infection of the jaw.

It's known that, during the princes' last days in the Tower, a doctor was brought in to treat Edward for a toothache. He reported that the boy "sought remission of his sins by daily confession and penance, because he believed that death was facing him." Perhaps he expected to be killed. Or it may be that, as the bones imply, he was deathly ill.

In Shakespeare's *Richard III*, Tyrell orders his men to carry out the murder, then denounces it as "The most arch deed of piteous massacre/That ever yet this land was guilty of."

There's still one troublesome fact that makes historians wonder whether the skeletons are really those of the princes: the chest containing them was found ten feet under the ground, beneath a set of stone steps. How could it have gotten there when the stairs were in place? Some scholars speculate that the bones were buried well before the Tower was built.

The
POET

IF THERE WERE ANY WITNESSES TO THE FATES of Tutankhamen or the princes in the Tower, they left no record of what they saw. Of course, when a statement from an eyewitness does exist, there's no way of knowing how accurate it is. Even witnesses who are doing their best to tell the truth inevitably forget things or remember them incorrectly. If they have some reason to lie, it makes matters even more uncertain.

We do have quite a detailed account of how Christopher Marlowe, the celebrated English playwright and poet, met his end on May 30, 1593. It's in the form of a coroner's report, based on the testimony of three rather shady characters who were with Marlowe when he died.

On the fateful day, the playwright and his companions gathered at a lodging house in Deptford, a suburb of London.

Opposite: This sixteenth-century painting, which hangs at Marlowe's alma mater, Cambridge University, is believed to be a portrait of the playwright.

17

The Tragicall Hiſtorie of the Life and Death of Doctor Fauſtus.

With new Additions.

Written by C H. M A R.

Printed at London for *Iohn Wright*, and are to be ſold at his ſhop without Newgate. 1631.

Probably Marlowe's most enduring work is his retelling of the legend of Faust, the scholar who sold his soul to the devil in exchange for knowledge.

They spent most of the day eating, drinking, and talking—about what, the report doesn't say. An argument broke out between Marlowe and a man named Ingram Frizer over who would pay the "reckoning"—the money they owed for food and drink. Marlowe snatched Frizer's dagger from his belt and struck him twice in the head, leaving two fairly minor cuts. Frizer seized the knife and "gave the said Christopher then & there a mortal wound over his right eye." The coroner ruled that Frizer had acted in self-defense, and he was pardoned.

Although Marlowe was only twenty-nine, he was already hailed as the greatest dramatist of his generation (Shakespeare hadn't made his mark yet), thanks to three extremely popular plays: *Tamburlaine the Great, Doctor Faustus,* and *The Jew of Malta.* Theatergoers were stunned by the news of his death. But few people were surprised; Marlowe was nearly as well known for his quick temper and reckless behavior as for his plays.

He had been in trouble of one sort or another since 1587, when he was a student at Cambridge University. His frequent unexplained absences from school made the faculty suspect that he was visiting a seminary in France, preparing to become a Catholic priest. This was a serious accusation; the priesthood had basically been outlawed by the Protestant Queen Elizabeth. When the university administrators tried to deny him his degree, they discovered that Marlowe had some very influential friends—namely the queen's Privy Council, made up of her closest advisers.

The council fired off a letter to Cambridge declaring that "it was not her majestie's pleasure that anie one emploied as [Marlowe] had been in matters touching the benefitt of his Countrie should be defamed by those that are ignorant in th'affaires he went about."

Marlowe had been working as a spy or a messenger in the service of Thomas Walsingham and his cousin, Sir Francis Walsingham, the queen's secretary of state. Sir Francis supervised a network of over fifty secret

Queen Elizabeth's fear of a Catholic conspiracy was more than mere paranoia. By 1586, her secret service had uncovered four major plots to overthrow or assassinate her.

agents whose task it was to foil Catholic conspiracies.

In 1589 Marlowe was involved in a sword fight that resulted in a man's death. He spent a couple of weeks in prison before he was acquitted. Two years later, a pair of constables (local law officers) asked the courts for a restraining order against the playwright, who had apparently threatened them. The following year, Marlowe was arrested on suspicion of "coining"—making counterfeit money. This was another serious charge, but thanks to his connections he escaped punishment.

A few weeks before his death he found himself in the worst predicament of his troubled career. In May, leaflets threatening violence against a recent spate of Dutch immigrants had begun appearing around London. One was in the form of a poem that contained references to Marlowe's work; it was signed "Tamburlaine." Marlowe was surely not so foolish as to incriminate himself this way; clearly someone was setting him up.

The Privy Council sent men to question Thomas Kyd, a playwright with whom Marlowe had once lodged. In Kyd's room they found a document containing "vile heretical conceits denying the deity of Jesus Christ our Saviour." After suffering "pains and undeserved tortures" at the hands of his captors, Kyd confessed that the blasphemous papers belonged to Marlowe and were just a sample of his "monstruous opinions" regarding religion.

There's no question that Marlowe had unconventional religious views. In fact, he was probably involved with Sir

Walter Raleigh's "School of Night," a circle of liberal thinkers that some called the School of Atheism because it attempted to apply scientific logic to religion.

But Marlowe and Kyd had not shared a room for two years, so it seems doubtful that the papers were Marlowe's. More likely it was another attempt to frame him. If so, it failed. The poet was brought before the Privy Council but, rather than being imprisoned and tortured, he was released with instructions to "give his daily attendance on their Lordships till he shall be licensed to the contrary."

Before he had a chance to plead his case before them, he was killed. It almost sounds as though someone didn't want him talking to the Privy Council—perhaps the same someone who penned the "Tamburlaine" tract and planted the heretical document.

Historians have nominated several suspects. One is the wife of Thomas Walsingham, Marlowe's patron. Lady Walsingham was reputedly involved in a plot to put Scotland's King James on the English throne. Marlowe had also considered shifting his loyalty to James. If the two were

It's not surprising that Marlowe would be drawn to Sir Walter Raleigh. Raleigh, too, was ambitious, adventurous, skeptical of organized religion, and as fond of fighting as he was of writing.

co-conspirators, Lady Walsingham undoubtedly feared that Marlowe would incriminate her. This theory is bolstered by the fact that Ingram Frizer, the man who killed Marlowe, was employed as a "business agent" by none other than Lady Walsingham.

Others point an accusing finger at Sir Walter Raleigh, who was once the queen's favorite but had now fallen out of favor. If Marlowe had inside information about the infamous School of Night and its members, Raleigh had good reason to want him kept quiet.

A third possible culprit is Raleigh's enemy and the queen's new favorite, the Earl of Essex. One of the men present at Marlowe's death was Nicholas Skeres, a sometime accomplice of Ingram Frizer. Skeres was a thief and a spy—and a servant of the Earl of Essex. According to one theory, Essex hoped that he could get Marlowe to betray Raleigh and his fellow "atheists" to the Privy Council. The meeting in Deptford presumably was an attempt by Skeres and Frizer to convince him. When Marlowe refused, they came to blows.

The Earl of Essex was so determined to bring down his rival, Raleigh, that he may have sabotaged Raleigh's efforts to establish a colony in the New World.

DEBATABLE DEATHS

The most intriguing—and most unlikely—scenario is that Marlowe faked his death in order to escape his troubles and his enemies: he fled England, but went on writing plays for the London stage under an assumed name—William Shakespeare.

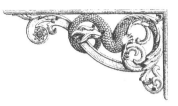

The COMPOSER

IT'S NOT HARD TO IMAGINE THE MURDER of a prince or a pharaoh. Every political regime and royal family in history has had its share of deadly enemies and desperate rivals. But why would anyone want to put a premature end to the life and career of a man who gave the world some of the most brilliant and delightful music ever written?

Since Wolfgang Amadeus Mozart was only thirty-five when he died, it's fortunate that he got such an early start. He was born in Austria in 1756 and began playing the harpsichord at age four. The following year he wrote two minuets for the instrument. A year later he was performing for the Austrian emperor. At seven he composed his first sonata; at eight, his first symphony; at twelve, his first opera.

Unlike many child prodigies, Mozart more than lived up to his early promise. He was both extremely popular and

Opposite: When this portrait was painted, Mozart was twenty-four and at a low point in his career. He was no longer a child prodigy, but he hadn't yet made his mark as a composer.

25

After hearing Allegri's *Miserere* performed only once, a teenaged Mozart wrote out the entire score of the choral work from memory.

extremely prolific. In 1787 the emperor appointed him court composer. Unfortunately, the salary was so small that he and his wife and children were continually plagued by debt; he was often reduced to begging friends to loan him money.

Though hardly anyone would have envied his financial situation, Mozart was envied for his musical genius, particularly by a composer named Antonio Salieri. Salieri seemingly had little reason to be jealous. He was well known and respected, both as a composer and as a teacher of such future luminaries as Beethoven, Schubert, and Liszt. But he was also, in the words of one writer of the time, "an insufferable egoist. He wants successes . . . only for his own operas . . . He is an enemy of all composers."

In 1782 he had done his best to block the production of Mozart's opera *The Abduction from the Seraglio.* But thanks to the intervention of the emperor himself, the piece was performed and was a great success—which of course only made Salieri more resentful. Three years later he tried to sabotage *The Marriage of Figaro* by convincing the performers Mozart had hired that the opera was unsingable. Again he failed. The cast and musicians were "intoxicated with pleasure" by the music.

By the time *The Magic Flute* premiered in September

1791, Salieri had either gotten over his jealousy or was very good at hiding it. He and Mozart actually attended the opera together, and Mozart reported that "Salieri listened and watched most attentively . . . There was not a single number that did not call forth from him a *bravo!*"

Whether Salieri knew it or not, he would soon be rid of his rival. In November, Mozart unexpectedly fell ill. According to an early Mozart biographer, "It began with swelling in his hands and feet and an almost total inability to move; this was followed by sudden vomiting." On December 5, the great composer died.

The cause of death was officially listed as "acute miliary fever." Many historians now believe that the composer was suffering from kidney disease, which produces the sorts of symptoms recorded by Mozart's doctors and friends. Others interpret those symptoms as evidence of rheumatic fever—which Mozart seems to have had in his youth—or of a streptococcal infection. A professor of medicine at the University of Washington blames undercooked pork chops, which could have given the composer a case of trichinosis.

Mozart himself felt he was a victim of something more sinister. Several weeks before he died he told his wife, "Someone has given me *acqua toffana* and has calculated the precise time of my death." *Acqua tof-*

If Salieri did have a hand in the great composer's death, Mozart's wife was apparently unaware of it. When her son, Franz, began to show musical talent, she engaged Salieri as his teacher.

In the last months of his life, Mozart accepted a commission to write a requiem, or mass for the dead. As he lay dying, friends gathered at his bedside to perform a selection from the unfinished piece.

fana was an arsenic-based poison.

This could be dismissed as a delusion brought on by his fever, except that several other sources expressed the same suspicion. After Mozart's funeral, a Berlin newspaper reported, "Because his body swelled up after death, some people even thought he had been poisoned." Mozart's son also noted how bloated his father's body was, so much so that no autopsy was performed. The corpse was unusually soft and flexible, too—another condition associated with poisoning.

The obvious suspect was, of course, the envious Salieri. He didn't help his cause by declaring that Mozart's death was a blessing for other composers; if Mozart had lived, he said, "not a soul would have given us a crust of bread for our work." By 1824 his guilt was so generally accepted that a concert program pictured him "standing by [Mozart's] side with the poisoned cup."

Around the same time, it was widely reported that Salieri, now an old man, had confessed to the murder and, filled with remorse, attempted suicide by cutting his throat. According to one of Salieri's pupils, however, the composer told him, "I assure you in good faith that there is no truth to that absurd rumor. Mozart, you know—I am supposed to have poisoned him. But no, it's malice, nothing but malice."

Even if Salieri was innocent, it doesn't rule out the possibility of poison. A number of scholars have speculated that Mozart was murdered by the Freemasons, a secret brotherhood to which the composer belonged. One theory is that the Masons were taking revenge on Mozart because he revealed too much about their mysterious rituals in his allegorical opera, *The Magic Flute*. This seems doubtful; the opera was written as a defense of Freemasonry, not an exposé.

A more credible culprit is Mozart's fellow Mason, Franz Hofdemel. The day after the composer's death, Hofdemel had a violent quarrel with his young wife, Maria, who may have been one of Mozart's piano students. Hofdemel slashed her face and torso with a razor, then killed himself. Although Maria refused to reveal what had provoked the attack, some said that she was romantically involved with her teacher and that Hofdemel had found out. There's no real evidence of this, but it does seem possible in light of a comment once made by Mozart's sister—that her brother gave lessons only to girls he was in love with.

In 1983, a mock trial was held to examine the possible causes of the great composer's death. The audience concluded that it was murder, and most were convinced that the guilty party was the jealous husband, Franz Hofdemel.

The EXPLORER

THANKS TO MODERN FORENSIC TECHNIQUES, scientists can sometimes determine the cause of a person's death decades, even centuries, after the fact—if they have something to work with. In Mozart's case, they don't. He was buried in an unmarked grave with no friends or family present, so no one knows exactly where to find his bones.

We do know where to find the remains of Meriwether Lewis, co-captain of the famous Corps of Discovery that explored the Louisiana Purchase in 1804–1806. We even know what killed him. What we don't know is whether he died by his own hand or someone else's.

To really understand the circumstances surrounding Lewis's death, we need to begin in 1808, the year before he died. President Thomas Jefferson had appointed Lewis governor of Upper Louisiana Territory. Although by most

Opposite:
As co-captain of the Corps of Discovery, Meriwether Lewis proved courageous, decisive, and self-assured. But friends noted that, when the expedition was over, he became more solitary and depressed.

accounts Lewis was an able administrator, he ran into financial problems. It all started when he outfitted an expedition for the purpose of returning a visiting Mandan chief to his people. Lewis submitted his expenses to the War Department, which refused to honor two of the bills, amounting to five hundred dollars.

The governor was already some four thousand dollars in debt. When his creditors heard about the contested bills, they demanded their money. Facing financial ruin, Lewis decided to travel to Washington to set things right. Judging from a letter he wrote to the secretary of war, there was more at stake than just money: "I have been informed [that] representations have been made against me. . . . Be assured, Sir, that my country can never make 'a Burr' of me. She may reduce me to poverty, but she can never sever my attachment to her."

He was referring to Aaron Burr, the former vice president. Burr was implicated in a scheme to take over the territory west of the Mississippi River and turn it into a separate nation. Apparently someone had accused Lewis of similar ambitions, and suggested that the expedition he'd sent out was meant to do more than just return the Mandan chief, that its real purpose was to explore the Western territory.

Some historians feel that Lewis may have had yet another motive for going to Washington: to present evidence against General James Wilkinson, the former governor of Louisiana, now the military commander of New

DEBATABLE DEATHS

Within two decades after Lewis's death, hundreds of steam-powered paddle wheelers would be plying the Mississippi. Lewis had to be content with a flatboat, pushed along by men with poles.

Orleans. Wilkinson was one of Aaron Burr's co-conspirators. In addition, he'd been selling sensitive information to the Spanish government for years.

Lewis left St. Louis by boat on September 4, 1809. He took along four trunks of personal belongings, including the notebooks he'd kept on his historic journey to the Pacific. Accompanying him was a servant whom Lewis called Pernia. Most scholars believe the man's name was John Pernier. They planned to float down to New Orleans, then board a ship for Washington.

But Lewis fell ill and had to be carried ashore at Fort Pickering, near present-day Memphis, Tennessee. Captain Gilbert Russell, the fort's commander, reported that Lewis was "in a state of mental derangement" and, according to the boatmen, "had made several attempts to put an end to his existence." But Lewis dosed himself with medicines and "on the sixth or seventh day all symptoms of derangement disappeared and he was completely in his senses." It sounds as though he may merely have been suffering another bout of the malaria he had contracted two years earlier.

While he was laid up, Lewis changed his travel plans. He decided to go by horseback along a trail known as the Natchez Trace. War with England was imminent and Lewis feared that, if he went by ship, the British might intercept him and confiscate his valuable journals. Of course, if he had damaging evidence against Wilkinson, that was another excellent reason to steer clear of New Orleans.

The Natchez Trace had long been the haunt of highwaymen who robbed, and sometimes murdered, solitary travelers. But Lewis had his servant for reinforcement. In addition, Major James Neelly, a Chickasaw Indian agent, had volunteered to accompany them, bringing his slave along. According to Captain Russell, several Chickasaws also rode with them.

In truth, Lewis might have been better off alone. Neelly's character seems questionable at best. Certainly Captain Russell disliked and distrusted him. So did the gov-

Although General Wilkinson was involved in Aaron Burr's plot to create an independent republic of Western states, he later testified against Burr. In 1811, Wilkinson was cleared of all charges of treason.

DEBATABLE DEATHS

ernment, which later dismissed him because of "hostility to the Indians." He was also, as you will see, a thief. It's interesting to note, too, that he owed his appointment as Indian agent to none other than the notorious General Wilkinson.

For over a week the group traveled together. On the morning of October 10, 1809, two of the packhorses ran off. Neelly and the Indians remained behind to round them up. Lewis and the servants went on ahead, Neelly later recalled, "with a promise to wait for me at the first house he Came to that was inhabited by white people."

Late in the day Lewis came upon a small settlement known as Grinder's Stand, consisting of two log cabins and a stable or barn. The Grinder family lived in one cabin and rented the other out to travelers. Lewis was greeted by Priscilla Grinder; her husband, Robert, she said, was tending a farm they owned some distance away.

She prepared a meal, but Lewis was too agitated to eat much. He strode about, "speaking to himself in a violent manner," perhaps rehearsing what he would say to the War Department. After dark the servants retired to the stable and Lewis to the guest cabin, where he went on pacing back and forth for hours, talking aloud "like a lawyer."

It's hard to know for certain exactly what happened next. Our only source of information is Priscilla Grinder, and she didn't write down her testimony. We have to depend on what other people claimed that she told them. One of these was Major Neelly, who can hardly be considered reliable.

Meriwether Lewis Park, near Hohenwald, Tennessee, features a replica of one of the log cabins at Grinder's Stand.

When Neelly arrived at the stand, Governor Lewis was already dead. In a letter to Thomas Jefferson, Neelly related what Mrs. Grinder supposedly told him: "About three oClock She heard two pistols fire off in the Governors Room; the Servants being awakined by her, came in but too late to save him, he had shot himself in the head with one pistol, & a little below the Breast with the other—when his Servant came in he says; I have done the business my good Servant give me some water. . . . he Survived but a short time." From Mrs. Grinder's account and from his own observations Neelly concluded that Lewis was "mentally deranged" and had taken his own life.

But by the time ornithologist Alexander Wilson visited the stand in 1811, Mrs. Grinder was telling her story quite differently. In this version, she "heard the report of a pistol, and something fall heavily to the floor, and the words 'O Lord!' Immediately afterwards she heard another pistol, and in a few minutes she heard him at her door calling out, 'O madam! give me some water and heal my wounds!'" Terrified, she ignored his plea. Lewis staggered back to his cabin. At daybreak, she fetched the servants from the stable. "They found him lying on the bed. . . . a piece of his forehead was blown off . . . He begged they would take his rifle and blow out his brains and he would give them all the money he had in his trunk. He often said, 'I am no coward; but I am so strong, so hard to die.'"

Nearly thirty years later a schoolteacher who stopped at the Grinders' got yet another version, with several new and intriguing elements: "About dark two or three other men rode up and called for lodging. Mr. Lewis immediately drew a brace of pistols, stepped towards them and challenged them to fight a duel. They not liking this salutation, rode on to the next house." The rest of the account is similar to the one Wilson heard except that, when Mrs. Grinder went to get the servants, she found that "Mr. P[ernia] had on the clothes Mr. L[ewis] wore when they came . . . and Mr. L's gold watch in his pocket. . . . Mr. P. and [Neelly's] servant then searched for Mr. L., found him and brought him to the house, and though he had on a full suit of clothes, they were old and tattered, and not the same as he had on the evening before."

This version implies that Pernia stole his master's watch and clothing—presumably after Lewis was dead—and that Lewis's body was found not in the cabin but somewhere on the grounds. It also implies that Lewis felt threatened by the unidentified men.

Historians have drawn all sorts of conclusions from this conflicting and ambiguous information. Some think that

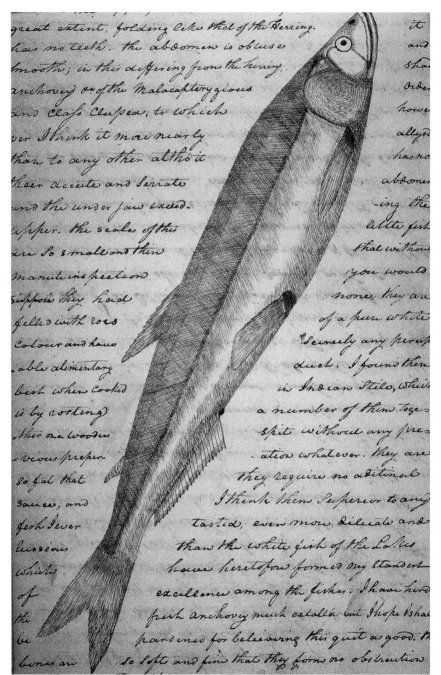

One thing Lewis meant to do during his trip back East was to organize the journals he'd kept during the expedition and get them in shape to be published.

the strangers were outlaws who returned later to rob and kill Lewis. This seems very possible; although Lewis was carrying at least two hundred dollars, the money was never found. Others suspect that Pernia was the thief, or perhaps Neelly; both claimed that the governor owed them money. One thing is certain: Neelly kept Lewis's firearms and his horse. Inhabitants of the area around Grinder's Stand have long believed that the culprit was Robert Grinder, who apparently had a reputation for violent behavior.

Some less obvious scenarios have also been suggested. One is that General Wilkinson, worried that Lewis would expose him as a traitor, sent an assassin after him. There's also a legend that says Lewis had discovered a gold mine during the expedition to the Pacific and was carrying a map that showed its location; if that story got around, there might have been dozens of people eager to rob him.

Of course there's no shortage of scholars who subscribe to the suicide theory. And it's true that a good deal of the evidence points that way. But Governor Lewis was very experienced in the use of firearms; it's hard to imagine why, if he really meant to kill himself, he would botch the job so badly.

Lewis's grave site at Grinder's Stand is now a national monument. Since 1996, James E. Starrs, a professor of forensic science, has been trying to convince the National Park Service to let him dig up the grave and examine the explorer's remains. Although Starrs has the support of 160 descendants of the Lewis family, the Park Service has so far refused permission.

The Death of Sacagawea

MERIWETHER LEWIS wasn't the only member of the Corps of Discovery to meet a questionable end. There's some doubt, too, about the fate of Sacagawea, the young Shoshone woman who helped guide Lewis and his co-captain, William Clark, provided them with wild foods, and eased their relations with Native Americans.

She and her husband, Toussaint Charbonneau, accompanied Lewis and Clark all the way to the Pacific. On the return trip, they left the company at Fort Mandan, in what is now North Dakota. Several months later, Sacagawea paid a visit to Clark in St. Louis.

When she returned to her people the following year, she left behind her two-year-old son, Jean-Baptiste, to be educated.

In December 1812, a clerk at Fort Manuel, a fur-trading post on the Yellowstone River, noted in his diary, "This evening the wife of Charbonneau, a Snake squaw, died of a putrid fever. She was . . . the best woman in the fort, aged about twenty-five years"— roughly the age Sacagawea would have been.

When Clark received the news, he thought at first that the woman might be another of Charbonneau's wives. But as the years passed and he heard nothing from Sacagawea, he came to believe that she was the woman the clerk had described. On a list of Corps members, he wrote next to her name, "Dead."

A century later, when Dr. Charles Eastman was interviewing members of several Plains Indian tribes, he found some who claimed to have known Sacagawea. Not only had she not died in 1812, they said, she had lived another seventy years or so. Eastman gathered that Sacagawea had left Charbonneau at some point and, after many years of wandering from tribe to tribe, ended up at Fort Washakie on the Shoshone reservation, where she was reunited with her son. According to Reverend John Roberts, who ministered to the Shoshones, she died in 1884. Though she would have been about ninety-six, according to Roberts she was "wonderfully active and intelligent . . . She walked alone and was bright to the last."

Opposite: Though Sacagawea was valuable as a guide and interpreter, her greatest contribution may have been keeping the peace. Because Lewis and Clark's party included a woman and a baby, the Indians they encountered were more inclined to be friendly.

The EMPEROR

IF THE TESTIMONY OF EYEWITNESSES IS questionable, and if the evidence provided by bones and mummified remains can be interpreted in so many different ways, can we ever hope to know for certain how a historical figure died? Well, what if doctors performed an autopsy soon after the subject's death and left a written report? That would seem to rule out any possibility of doubt, wouldn't it?

Not necessarily. After exiled French emperor Napoleon Bonaparte died on May 5, 1821, at the age of fifty-one, his body was dissected and examined by his personal physician in the presence of six other doctors. They found that Napoleon had a cancerous stomach ulcer. According to their report, "the diseased state of the stomach was the sole cause of death." But a number of modern historians believe

Opposite: In despair after his abdication, Napoleon attempted suicide by swallowing a mixture of opium, belladonna, and white hellebore. The combination was so nauseating that he promptly threw it up.

43

that the doctors were mistaken—or that perhaps they were simply telling British authorities what they wanted to hear.

Napoleon came to power during the French Revolution and declared himself emperor in 1804. Not content to rule France, he began invading neighboring countries. In 1814, an alliance of European countries finally defeated him in battle. He was forced to abdicate and was exiled to the island of Elba. A year later he made a triumphant return to France, only to be defeated by the allies again and banished again, this time to Saint Helena, a small, British-controlled island off the west coast of Africa.

An English doctor described Saint Helena as "the ugliest and most dismal rock conceivable." The climate was equally dismal, so damp that the walls of Napoleon's residence were covered with mold. The dreary house was also infested with rats, which scurried about under the table during meals.

Although Napoleon's family was not allowed to accompany him, he brought a dozen attendants, including a former member of his court, the comte de Montholon. For a time life was tolerable. Napoleon's health was good. He ate well, went riding when the weather allowed, and received a steady stream of visitors.

Then, in April 1816, Sir Hudson Lowe, the new governor of Saint Helena, arrived. Fearing an escape attempt, Lowe treated his charge more like a prisoner than a deposed head of state. Napoleon's freedom was restricted; his visitors were screened; his mail was censored. Lowe refused to deliver any gifts addressed to "the emperor." He also reduced the amount of money allotted to Napoleon's household for food and upkeep.

Napoleon was convinced that Lowe had been sent not to guard him but to kill him. He referred to the governor as "that hired assassin." His accusations may have had some basis in fact. According to historian David Hamilton-Williams, the British government had for years been financing a secret organization whose purpose was to get rid of Napoleon. The organization was headed by the comte d'Artois, who later ruled France as King Charles X.

There's no real evidence that Lowe was part of this plot. But one of Napoleon's physicians reported hearing the governor speak of "the benefit which would result to Europe from the death of Napoleon." And it does seem curious, to say the least, that, almost from the day Lowe arrived on Saint Helena, the emperor's health began to decline. In May he complained of weakness in his legs, headaches,

When Charles X tried to undo the changes brought on by the French Revolution, his policies so angered the people that he was forced to abdicate. Like Napoleon, he died in exile.

Governor Lowe was every bit as disagreeable as he appears in this portrait.

Above: Lowe searched Napoleon's papers, looking for escape plans, but found none.
Below: Though Napoleon repeatedly protested the limitations imposed by Lowe, the governor refused to relent.

chills, and a sharp pain in his side. He was sensitive to light; his speech was slurred and his behavior was lethargic, as though he'd been drugged.

Lowe was certain that Napoleon was faking his symptoms, in the hope that he'd be transferred to some more civilized place. A naval surgeon who was brought in diagnosed the illness as hepatitis, an inflammation of the liver. This seems like a good possibility; it was a common cause of death on Saint Helena. But Lowe dismissed this opinion—which implied that the emperor should be moved to more healthy surroundings—and had the surgeon court-martialed. He was replaced by an Italian physician, Francesco Antommarchi, who examined Napoleon and obligingly concluded that "the patient's condition does not suggest any immediate danger."

But Napoleon continued to have severe bouts of fever and nausea, and a pain in his side "like a gentle thrust from a sharp blade." For a time he insisted that he was being poisoned, "murdered by the English oligarchy and its hired assassin." Later he became convinced that he was dying of the same disease that had killed his father—stomach cancer.

The autopsy report seems to confirm this. What it does not reveal is that there was a difference of opinion among the doctors who were present. One of them pointed out that Napoleon's liver was enlarged, a condition that might indicate hepatitis—or perhaps poison. His observation did not make it into the report, possibly because Governor Lowe objected.

Napoleon was not allowed to escape the island even in death. He was buried there. Nineteen years later, some of his countrymen came to dig up the grave and return his remains to France. When they opened the coffin, they found that the body was perfectly preserved. Since high levels of arsenic slow down the decomposition process, some saw this as evidence that Napoleon had, indeed, been poisoned.

More than a century passed, though, before anyone bothered to actually test for arsenic. Several locks of Napoleon's hair have survived. In 1960 a Swedish toxicologist tested one of the hair samples. He found it contained "relatively large amounts of arsenic." His theory was that Napoleon's seemingly devoted companion, the comte de Montholon, was actually in the service of the comte d'Artois, the heir to the French throne, and that Montholon had secretly poisoned the emperor's wine supply.

In 1980 Dr. David Jones, a British chemist, proposed a

After Napoleon grew ill, he had his bed moved into the drawing room pictured here. The color and pattern of the wallpaper match the sample tested by Dr. Jones.

less sinister possibility. After testing a scrap of wallpaper taken from the room in which Napoleon died, he concluded that the pigment used to color the paper was Scheele's Green, which was made from copper arsenite. When the wallpaper grew damp and moldy, it would have given off a vapor poisonous enough to make the room's occupants seriously ill.

More recent findings indicate that this may not have been the only source of arsenic Napoleon was exposed to. A police lab in Paris tested samples of the emperor's hair collected *before* his exile on Saint Helena and found that

DEBATABLE DEATHS

they, too, showed dangerously high levels of the toxic element. Some scientists suggest that Napoleon may, in fact, have been unwittingly poisoning himself for years, by using one of the nineteenth-century hair-restoring tonics that contained arsenic.

The AVIATOR

SCHOLARS HAVE BEEN ARGUING LITERALLY for centuries about the fates of Meriwether Lewis and Christopher Marlowe and the princes in the Tower. But none of those long-debated deaths has generated as much controversy or speculation as a case that took place less than seventy years ago: the disappearance of Amelia Earhart. Chances are someone in your family can recall hearing about it on the radio or reading about it in a newspaper. It was, in the words of author Mike Campbell, "one of the most publicized—and mispublicized—stories of the 20th century."

Air travel is such a commonplace thing these days, such an ordinary part of our lives, that it's hard to imagine a pilot achieving celebrity status. But when Amelia Earhart began her career in the 1920s, flying was still something of a nov-

Opposite: Amelia Earhart was planning to study medicine at Columbia University, but then she took her first airplane ride and was struck by a "sense of the inevitability of flying."

elty, and pilots were considered daring pioneers. Charles Lindbergh's solo nonstop flight across the Atlantic in 1927 made him a hero and a household name.

A year later Earhart was the first woman to cross the Atlantic by air. Although she was only a passenger—a "sack of potatoes," as she put it—the flight made her famous. She proceeded to add to her reputation. She set a world speed record for women pilots. She was the first woman to fly solo across the Atlantic and the first to fly nonstop across North America. She was the first pilot, male or female, to fly alone from Hawaii to the mainland and from Mexico City to New York. She was also an outspoken champion of women's rights who spoke of a day "when women will know no restrictions because of sex but

Earhart smiles confidently for the camera before setting out on her 1935 solo flight from Hawaii to the mainland.

will be individuals free to live their lives as men are free."

By the time she was forty, Earhart was one of the best known and most admired women in the world. But she wasn't content to rest on her laurels. She wanted to make a last epic journey, one that would assure her a place in aviation history: a 25,000-mile flight around the world.

Famed pilot Wiley Post had already circumnavigated the globe twice. Earhart was determined to be the first woman to accomplish the feat. "I have a feeling," she told a reporter, "that there is just about one more good flight left in my system and I hope this trip is it. Anyway when I have finished this job, I mean to give up long-distance 'stunt' flying."

Initially she planned to make the flight alone, but, realizing that her navigational skills weren't up to the task, she took on an experienced navigator, Harry Manning. Her aircraft, a twin-engine Lockheed Electra, was outfitted with extra fuel tanks that gave her a range of 2,500 to 3,000 miles. But the distance across the Pacific from North America to New Guinea was 7,000 miles. Luckily the United States was about to build an airstrip on tiny Howland Island, roughly halfway across the ocean, and Earhart got permission to use it.

To shorten the distance even more, she made a stop in Hawaii. As she was taking off on the second leg of the journey, the plane veered sideways. Accustomed to handling a lighter, single-engine craft, Earhart turned too quickly in the other direction. Under the strain the landing gear collapsed.

Even after her first attempt at circumnavigating the globe failed, Earhart seems cheerful and confident. So does the "happy-go-lucky" Fred Noonan, on her left. Only Harry Manning looks grim.

Earhart blamed the incident on faulty equipment and, confident about her own skills, made a second attempt at a round-the-world flight on May 20, 1937, flying east this time from Oakland, California. Harry Manning, her chief navigator, wasn't on board. He declared that he was "fed up with her bull-headedness . . . She really had an ego, and could be tough as nails." Although his replacement, Fred Noonan, had plenty of experience, Manning considered him "a happy-go-lucky Irishman. He wasn't a 'constant' navigator." Noonan also had a problem with alcohol.

Making a series of short flights, it took Earhart and Noonan more than a month to get across North and South America, Africa, and southern Asia. By the time they reached New Guinea, the strain had begun to take its toll on them. Earhart was exhausted and Noonan was drinking heavily. They rested for two days and, on the morning of July 2, took off for Howland Island. Because of a strong headwind, they were using fuel at a much faster rate than they'd anticipated. By the time they reached Howland,

DEBATABLE DEATHS

they would be running on empty. If they somehow missed the island, they were in trouble. The plane was equipped with a two-way radio and a direction finder. The problem was, neither the pilot nor the navigator knew how to operate them properly.

The Coast Guard cutter *Itasca* waited off Howland Island to help guide them in. But Earhart mistakenly used too high a frequency for her transmissions, and the Coast Guard radioman could barely hear them. There was also some confusion about what time transmissions were to be made, so Earhart failed to receive most of the *Itasca*'s messages.

The plane never reached Howland. If Noonan was hungover and not thinking clearly, he may have made an error in his calculations. Even if he gave Earhart the correct bearing, she may have ignored him, preferring to trust her instincts. She had done that very thing before, when they were crossing the Atlantic, and ended up some one hundred miles north of their intended destination.

Nineteen hours after Earhart left New Guinea, the *Itasca* got a clear message from her: "We must be on you but cannot see you but gas is running low." An hour later she radioed, "We are on the line of position one five seven dash three three seven. . . . We are running north and south." That was the last anyone heard from her—officially, anyway.

The Coast Guard and navy conducted a search that covered 250,000 square miles of ocean but found no sign of the plane or its crew. Some speculated that when Earhart real-

Though a number of radio operators reported receiving messages from Earhart after her plane went down, the Coast Guard dismissed all the reports as false.

ized she couldn't reach Howland, she turned north in the hope of making an emergency landing in the Gilbert Islands. A search of that area turned up nothing. No attempt was made to search the Marshall Islands, which lay north of the Gilberts. They were controlled by the Japanese, who were being very secretive about what went on there. The United States government suspected—correctly, as it turned out—that Japan was developing the islands for military use.

When the United States went to war with Japan four years later, a rumor surfaced that Earhart's flight had had a dual purpose—that, since she was flying so close to Japanese territory, President Roosevelt had asked her to do a bit of spying. The rumor was fueled by the release of a movie titled *Flight for Freedom,* the story of a woman pilot who deliberately goes down in the Pacific just so the United States can conduct a search and, in the process, check out what the Japanese are up to. Even Earhart's mother declared, "I am convinced she was on some sort of

56

government mission." The navy issued an emphatic denial. So did Eleanor Roosevelt, the First Lady.

In 1960 a woman named Josephine Blanco Akiyama, who grew up on Saipan, in the Japanese-controlled Mariana Islands, made a startling revelation. In the summer of 1937 she had seen a twin-engine plane land in Saipan harbor. Japanese soldiers brought ashore an American woman with short hair, dressed in men's clothing, accompanied by a tall man. The two were taken into the woods; Akiyama heard shots, then the soldiers returned without the prisoners.

Others came forward with stories that seemed to confirm Akiyama's, but, as invariably happens with eyewitnesses, the details of their accounts differed. An army sergeant stationed on Saipan in 1944–1945, when American forces controlled the island, recalled seeing an aircraft that matched the Lockheed's description in a hangar there. When he asked the guard if the plane was Earhart's, the man replied, "Yes, but for the love of God don't say I said so." Later, a local woman showed him the grave of two white people who had "come from the sky" and been captured and killed by the Japanese.

This map shows the location of Lae, New Guinea (#1), the starting point for the flight across the Pacific; Howland Island (#2), where the plane was to refuel; and Saipan (#3), where witnesses reported seeing a captured woman pilot.

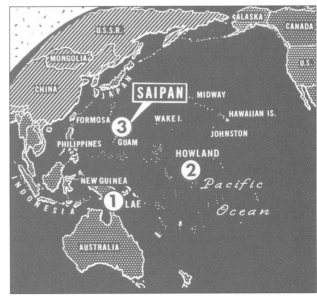

A former Japanese medical corpsman also saw a plane that would seem to be Earhart's, but it was being transported on the deck of a Japanese ship. The medic had been brought aboard the ship to tend to two injured English-speaking prisoners. "Crew called lady, 'Meel-ya,'" he later recalled. "Japanese officer tell me ship go to Saipan." This version indicates that Earhart and Noonan landed somewhere other than Saipan. According to an official of the Marshallese government, "There's no question they went down in the Marshalls. Lot of people saw them."

But a lot of other people aren't convinced. In 1970 author Joe Klaas claimed that a New Jersey woman named Irene Bolam was actually Amelia Earhart. Bolam, who did in fact resemble Earhart, vehemently denied the charge.

The International Group for Historic Aircraft Recovery (TIGHAR) believes that Earhart ended up south of

Howland and crash-landed on or near Gardner Island, now called Nikumaroro. TIGHAR has sent several expeditions to explore the island. They've turned up some assorted debris, including a size nine shoe (according to Earhart's family, the aviator wore a size six or six-and-a-half) and an aluminum bookcase, but nothing conclusive.

In 2002, Nauticos Corporation, the team that located the *Titanic,* spent six weeks sweeping the ocean floor near Howland Island with a sonar device, but found no trace of Earhart's plane.

The *New Haven Register* once asked its readers, "What do you think happened to Amelia Earhart?" Here are some of their replies:

"My guess is she probably crashed and died somewhere."

"I believe Earhart and Noonan both were executed . . . on suspicion of espionage."

"Amelia Earhart is alive and well. In fact, informed sources say she said, 'Never mind me, find my luggage.'"

"I believe she was abducted by a UFO full of Elvis impersonators."

"I believe that she flew so high that she could never return to Earth. She's still up there with all the heroes and heroines of my childhood."

WORDS FOR THE WISE

Akhenaten (d. 1362 BCE) King of Egypt from the death of his father, Amenhotep III, in 1379 BCE until his own death. He left Thebes, the traditional seat of power, and built a new capital at Tell el-Amarna. After the death of his son and successor, Tutankhamen, the buildings were destroyed.

arsenic A metallic element that occurs in very small quantities in the earth's crust. It has been used to treat infections, to harden copper and lead, to kill insects—and, of course, to poison one's enemies.

direction finder A piece of equipment that enables pilots to get their bearings by homing in on radio signals transmitted from the ground.

Edward IV (1442–1483) King of England from 1461, when he deposed Henry VI, until his death (except for the time when Henry took the throne back for a year). Edward and his relatives were of the House of York; Henry's family were of the House of Lancaster. The two factions fought over the crown for three decades—a conflict known as the Wars of the Roses—until Henry Tudor (see Henry VII) became king.

Essex, Earl of (1567–1601) Robert Devereux, second earl of Essex, a handsome, dashing soldier, became the favorite companion of Queen Elizabeth I, despite the fact that he was far younger than she was. After a failed military campaign against Ireland, he fell out of favor. He tried to lead a rebellion against the queen and was beheaded.

Freemasons A worldwide fraternal order, begun in London in 1717, that promotes harmony and service to others. It probably evolved from the medieval guild of stonemasons and uses the mason's tools as its symbols.

French Revolution (1789–1799) A violent uprising sparked by many factors, including food shortages and the resentment of the growing middle class toward the aristocracy. In 1792, revolutionary forces deposed King Louis XVI and declared the country a republic. Napoleon Bonaparte, the commander of the army, was chosen to head the new government.

Henry VII (1457–1509) King of England from 1485 until his death. Henry (who, although his surname was Tudor, was a Lancaster) reconciled the warring houses of Lancaster and York by marrying Elizabeth of York—daughter of Edward IV and sister of the princes in the Tower.

Hittites An ancient group of related peoples who spoke an Indo-European language (Egypt's language is classified as Afro-Asiatic). Around 1600 BCE they destroyed the city of Babylon and went on to establish a powerful empire that included most of modern-day Turkey and Syria. It was, in turn, destroyed by invaders around 1200 BCE.

Kyd, Thomas (1558–1594) Playwright best known for *The Spanish Tragedy*, the most popular play of the Elizabethan theater until Marlowe came along.

Magic Flute, The (Die Zauberflote) Mozart's final opera, about a prince who is asked by the Queen of the Night to rescue her daughter from a cruel magician. Although the fanciful story, which is laced with Masonic symbolism, is a bit hard to follow, the music is memorable.

Marshall Islands A group of thirty-four islands located 2,200 miles southwest of Hawaii. The Marshalls were Japanese territory from

1914 until 1944, when they were captured by the United States, which used them as a testing ground for atomic and hydrogen bombs.

More, Sir Thomas (1478–1535) Scholar and statesman who became lord chancellor of England. A staunch Catholic, he opposed King Henry VIII's divorce and refused to recognize Henry as head of the Church of England. More was found guilty of treason and beheaded. In 1935, the Catholic Church declared him a saint.

Natchez Trace A road that traversed five hundred miles of wilderness between Natchez, Mississippi, and Nashville, Tennessee. The United States Army began clearing the route in 1801, following an old Indian trail.

New Guinea The second largest island in the world, located just north of Australia. In 1937, the island was controlled by Australia. Today, the western half is a province of Indonesia; the eastern half is the nation of Papua New Guinea.

oligarchy Greek for "rule by the few," the term refers to a government that is controlled by a small group, usually on the basis of class or military power.

Post, Wiley (1899–1935) Texas aviator who, with navigator Harold Gatty, flew around the world in July 1931. The trip took less than nine days. In 1933, Post made the trip solo and shaved a day off his time. Two years later, on a flight with humorist Will Rogers, Post crashed his plane in Alaska. Both men were killed.

Raleigh, Sir Walter (1552?–1618) English military commander and writer. A favorite courtier of Queen Elizabeth I, Raleigh incurred her displeasure by marrying one of her maids of honor. Elizabeth's successor, James I, suspected Raleigh of conspiring against him. He imprisoned Raleigh in the Tower of

London for thirteen years and finally had him executed.

Saipan The second largest of the Mariana Islands. Inhabited since about 1500 BCE, Saipan was discovered by Europeans in 1561 and fell under the control of Spain, then Germany, then Japan, then the United States.

trichinosis A parasitic disease caused by eating raw or under-cooked pork infected with the roundworm *Trichinella spiralis*.

LEARN MORE ABOUT DEBATABLE DEATHS

BOOKS

Lace, William W. *The Little Princes in the Tower.* Mysterious Deaths series. San Diego, CA: Lucent, 1997.

> A thorough, clear picture of the complex political situation sur-rounding the princes' deaths. Includes a chronology of events and family trees of the major figures. Although Lace seems con-vinced of Richard's guilt, he does discuss other possibilities.

Reeves, Nicholas. *Into the Mummy's Tomb: The Real-Life Discovery of Tutankhamun's Treasures.* A Time Quest Book. New York: Scholastic, 1992.

> Reeves—who himself found artifacts from Tutankhamen's tomb hidden in Lord Carnarvon's mansion—makes Carter's search for and discovery of the tomb into a riveting story. Features photos of the treasure, a diagram of the tomb, and a discussion of how mummies were made.

Szabo, Corinne. *Sky Pioneer.* Washington, DC: National Geographic, 1997.

> A concise account of Amelia Earhart's life and accomplishments, enhanced by plenty of photos, maps of her around-the-world

route, and excerpts from the aviator's own writings. An afterword discusses the various theories about her disappearance.

ONLINE INFORMATION*

www.ameliaearhartmuseum.org

Web site of the Amelia Earhart Birthplace Museum in Atchison, KS. Many photos of Earhart, information about her early years, plus short biographies of other women aviators.

www.marlowe-society.org

Everything you'd care to know about Christopher Marlowe, his plays, and his spying career, more about the Shakespeare hypothesis, and even a full transcript of the coroner's report.

www.mozartproject.org

Essays about the composer and his music, links to related sites.

www.tighar.org

Web site of The International Group for Historic Aircraft Recovery. The Earhart Project pages explain in detail why the group believes that Earhart landed on Nikumaroro. Photos, maps, logs of the expeditions, reviews of Earhart-related books and films, and film footage of Earhart's takeoff from New Guinea.

VIDEOS

Meriwether Lewis: Suicide or Murder? The History Channel's *In Search of History* series. A&E Television, 1999.

A rather stilted, documentary-style dramatization of the events, but accurate. The program raises many good questions, and discusses the most popular theories.

*All Internet sites were available and accurate when this book was sent to press.

BIBLIOGRAPHY

Ambrose, Stephen E. *Undaunted Courage: Meriwether Lewis, Thomas Jefferson, and the Opening of the American West.* New York: Simon & Schuster, 1996.

Aubry, Octave. *St. Helena.* Philadelphia: Lippincott, 1936.

Bakeless, John. *The Tragicall History of Christopher Marlowe.* Vol. 1. Westport, CT: Greenwood Press, 1970.

Ball, Hendrik. "The Strange Story of Napoleon's Wallpaper." http://www.grand-illusions.com/napoleon/napol3.htm

Borowitz, Albert. "Salieri and the 'Murder' of Mozart." *Legal Studies Forum* 27, no. 1 (2003): 185–201.

Braunbehrens, Volkmar. *Mozart in Vienna: 1781–1791.* New York: Grove Weidenfeld, 1986.

Brier, Bob, PhD. *The Murder of Tutankhamen: A True Story.* New York: Putnam, 1998.

"British 'Cleared' of Napoleon's Murder." http://news.bbc.co.uk/l/hi/sci/tech/2371187.stm

Campbell, Mike, with Thomas E. Devine. *With Our Own Eyes: Eyewitnesses to the Final Days of Amelia Earhart.* Lancaster, OH: Lucky Press, 2002.

Cross, Milton, and David Ewen. *The Milton Cross New Encyclopedia of the Great Composers and Their Music.* Garden City, NY: Doubleday, 1969.

"Did Bad Pork Chops Kill Mozart?" *Current Science* 87, no. 7 (November 23, 2001): 13.

Dillon, Richard. *Meriwether Lewis: A Biography.* New York: Coward-McCann, 1965.

"Earhart Overview" and "Earhart Project Hypothesis, November 2001." http://www.tighar.org/Projects/Earhart

Editors of Reader's Digest. *Great Mysteries of the Past: Experts Unravel Fact and Fallacy Behind the Headlines of History.* Pleasantville, NY: Reader's Digest, 1991.

Editors of Reader's Digest. *Mysteries of the Unexplained.* Pleasantville, NY: Reader's Digest, 1982.

El Mahdy, Christine. *Tutankhamen: The Life and Death of the Boy-King.* New York: St. Martin's, 1999.

Fisher, Vardis. *Suicide or Murder?: The Strange Death of Governor Meriwether Lewis.* Athens, OH: Swallow Press, 1962.

Hamilton-Williams, David. *The Fall of Napoleon: The Final Betrayal.* New York: Wiley, 1994.

Hoffman, Calvin. *The Murder of the Man Who Was "Shakespeare."* New York: Julian Messner, 1955.

Hotson, J. Leslie. *The Death of Christopher Marlowe.* New York: Russell & Russell, 1967.

Hoving, Thomas. *Tutankhamun: The Untold Story.* New York: Simon & Schuster, 1978.

Huntington, Tom. "On Her Majesty's Secret Service," *British Heritage* 24, no. 3 (May 2003): 18–24.

Long, Elgen M., and Marie K. Long. *Amelia Earhart: The Mystery Solved.* New York: Simon & Schuster, 1999.

Loomis, Vincent V., with Jeffrey L. Ethell. *Amelia Earhart: The Final Story.* New York: Random House, 1985.

Lovell, Mary S. *The Sound of Wings: The Life of Amelia Earhart.* New York: St. Martin's, 1989.

Mysteries of Mind Space & Time: The Unexplained. Vols. 7, 19. Westport, CT: H. S. Stuttman, 1992.

"Nauticos Makes Progress on Amelia Earhart Search."
  http://www.nauticos.com/news/news2002-05-16.html

Nicholl, Charles. *The Reckoning: The Murder of Christopher Marlowe.* New York: Harcourt Brace, 1992.

"Princes in the Tower."
  http://www.richardiii.net/richardiii_princes.htm

Sassaman, Richard. "The Meriwether Lewis Murder Mystery: Three Perspectives." *American History* 38, no. 2 (April 2003).

"Soundoff" column, *New Haven Register,* January 7, 1991.

Walker, Dale L. *Legends and Lies: Great Mysteries of the American West.* New York: Forge, 1997.

Weir, Alison. *The Princes in the Tower.* New York: Ballantine, 1992.

"Who Killed Meriwether Lewis?"
  http://www.salon.com/it/feature/1999/03/22feature.html

"Who Killed Tut?!!" http://www.sis.gov.eg/tut/html/tut04.htm

Williamson, Audrey. *The Mystery of the Princes: An Investigation into a Supposed Murder.* Totowa, NJ: Rowman and Littlefield, 1978.

NOTES ON QUOTES

INTRODUCTION

Page vii, "It is the questioners": Williamson, *The Mystery of the Princes: An Investigation into a Supposed Murder*, p. 199.

CHAPTER ONE: THE PHARAOH

Page 1, "the richest discovery": Hoving, *Tutankhamun: The Untold Story*, p. 11.

Page 2, "Perhaps the most": El Mahdy, *Tutankhamen: The Life and Death of the Boy-King*, p. 77.

Page 3, "My husband is dead": El Mahdy, *Tutankhamen: The Life and Death of the Boy-King*, p. 300.

Page 4, "arranged [Tutankhamen's] death": Brier, *The Murder of Tutankhamen: A True Story*, p. 148.

Page 4, "And this could have been": Brier, *The Murder of Tutankhamen*, p. xv.

Page 5, "Egyptian brothers": "Who Killed Tut?!!"

CHAPTER TWO: THE PRINCES

Page 9, "the bones of those": Weir, *The Princes in the Tower*, p. 252.

Page 10, "We can dig": Nicholl, *The Reckoning: The Murder of Christopher Marlowe*, p. 3.

Page 11, "bloody adherents": Williamson, *The Mystery of the Princes*, pp. 52–53.

Page 12, "virtuous disposition": Weir, *The Princes in the Tower*, p. 59.

Page 12, "began to support": Williamson, *The Mystery of the Princes*, p. 49.

Page 12, "that the children": Williamson, *The Mystery of the Princes*, p. 78.

Page 12, "were seen shotying": Williamson, *The Mystery of the Princes*, p. 95.

Page 12, "had died": Williamson, *The Mystery of the Princes*, p. 99.

Page 13, "at the stair foot": Weir, *The Princes in the Tower*, p. 159.

Page 13, "who had put": Williamson, *The Mystery of the Princes*, p. 101.

Page 14, "the bones": Weir, *The Princes in the Tower*, p. 159.

Page 14, "in a better place": Weir, *The Princes in the Tower*, p. 161.

Page 14, "living freely": Williamson, *The Mystery of the Princes*, p. 94.

Page 14, "the sons of Edward IV" and "some remain": Williamson, *The Mystery of the Princes*, p. 94.

Page 15, "sought remission": Williamson, *The Mystery of the Princes*, p. 116.

CHAPTER THREE: THE POET

Page 18, "gave the said Christopher": Bakeless, *The Tragicall History of*

Christopher Marlowe. Vol. 1, p. 156.

Page 19, "it was not": Bakeless, *The Tragicall History of Christopher Marlowe*, p. 77.

Page 20, "vile heretical conceits" and "pains and undeserved tortures": Nicholl, *The Reckoning*, p. 289.

Page 20, "monstruous opinions": Bakeless, *The Tragicall History of Christopher Marlowe*, p. 114.

Page 21, "give his daily": Hoffman, *The Murder of the Man Who Was "Shakespeare,"* p. 64.

CHAPTER FOUR: THE COMPOSER

Page 26, "an insufferable egoist": Borowitz, "Salieri and the 'Murder' of Mozart," p. 192.

Page 26, "intoxicated with pleasure": Cross and Ewen, *The Milton Cross Encyclopedia of the Great Composers and Their Music*, p. 649.

Page 27, "Salieri listened": Braunbehrens, *Mozart in Vienna: 1781–1791*, p. 394.

Page 27, "It began with," "acute miliary fever," and "Someone has given": Editors of Reader's Digest, *Great Mysteries of the Past: Experts Unravel Fact and Fallacy Behind the Headlines of History*, p. 98.

Page 28, "Because his body": Braunbehrens, *Mozart in Vienna*, p. 407.

Page 28, "not a soul": Editors of Reader's Digest, *Great Mysteries of the Past*, p. 100.

Page 28, "standing by [Mozart's] side": Borowitz, "Salieri and the 'Murder' of Mozart," p. 193.

Page 28, "I assure you": Braunbehrens, *Mozart in Vienna*, p. 409.

CHAPTER FIVE: THE EXPLORER

Page 32, "I have been informed": Dillon, *Meriwether Lewis: A Biography*, pp. 325-326.

Page 33, "in a state" and "had made several attempts": Walker, *Legends and Lies: Great Mysteries of the American West*, p. 57.

Page 34, "on the sixth": Ambrose, *Undaunted Courage: Meriwether Lewis, Thomas Jefferson, and the Opening of the American West*, p. 462.

Page 35, "hostility to the Indians": Walker, *Legends and Lies*, p. 58.

Page 35, "with a promise": Ambrose, *Undaunted Courage*, p. 463.

Page 35, "speaking to himself": Ambrose, *Undaunted Courage*, p. 463.

Page 35, "like a lawyer": Ambrose, *Undaunted Courage*, p. 465.

Page 36, "About three oClock": Fisher, *Suicide or Murder?: The Strange Death of Governor Meriwether Lewis*, p. 129.

Page 36, "heard the report" and "They found": Fisher, *Suicide or Murder?*, pp. 148–149.

Page 37, "About dark": Fisher, *Suicide or Murder?*, p. 155.

Page 37, "Mr. P[ernia] had": Fisher, *Suicide or Murder?*, p. 156.

CHAPTER SIX: THE EMPEROR

Page 43, "the diseased state": Aubry, *St. Helena*, p. 511.

Page 44, "the ugliest and most dismal": Editors of Reader's Digest, *Great Mysteries of the Past*, p. 125.

Page 45, "that hired assassin": Hamilton-Williams, *The Fall of Napoleon: The Final Betrayal*, p. 281.

Page 45, "the benefit which": Editors of Reader's Digest, *Great Mysteries of the Past*, p. 127.

Page 46, "the patient's condition": Aubry, *St. Helena*, p. 439.

Page 46, "like a gentle thrust": Aubry, *St. Helena*, p. 444.

Page 46, "murdered by the English": Hamilton-Williams, *The Fall of Napoleon*, p. 288.

Page 47, "relatively large amounts": Editors of Reader's Digest, *Great Mysteries of the Past*, p. 128.

CHAPTER SEVEN: THE AVIATOR

Page 51, "one of the most": Campbell, *With Our Own Eyes: Eyewitnesses to the Final Days of Amelia Earhart*, p. 201.

Page 52, "sack of potatoes": Long, *Amelia Earhart: The Mystery Solved*, p. 46.

Page 52, "when women will": Loomis, *Amelia Earhart: The Final Story*, p. 39.

Page 53, "I have a feeling": Lovell, *The Sound of Wings: The Life of Amelia Earhart*, p. 260.

Page 54, "fed up with" and "a happy-go-lucky Irishman": Lovell, *The Sound of Wings*, p. 255.

Page 55, "We must be on you": Lovell, *The Sound of Wings*, p. 282.

Page 55, "We are on the line": Lovell, *The Sound of Wings*, p. 285.

Page 56, "I am convinced": Campbell, *With Our Own Eyes*, p. 121.

Page 57, "Yes, but for": Campbell, *With Our Own Eyes*, p. 3.

Page 57, "come from the sky": Campbell, *With Our Own Eyes*, p. 9.

Page 58, "Crew called lady": Campbell, *With Our Own Eyes*, p. 145.

Page 58, "There's no question": Campbell, *With Our Own Eyes*, p. 149.

Page 59, "What do you think," "My guess is," etc.: "Soundoff" column, *New Haven Register*, January 7, 1991.

INDEX

Page numbers for illustrations are in boldface

ABOUT THE AUTHOR

GARY L. BLACKWOOD has long been fascinated both with history and with the mysterious, so it's only natural that he should combine the two—not only in this set of books but in many of his other works, including the nonfiction series SECRETS OF THE UNEXPLAINED, and the historical novels *The Shakespeare Stealer*, *The Year of the Hangman*, and *Second Sight*.